Profiles of Integrity

1

Real People
Who Demonstrated
Godly Character

Marilyn Boyer &
Grace Tumas Ehrman

Master Books First Printing: January 2026

Master Books, P.O. Box 726, Green Forest, AR 72638

Master Books® is a division of
the New Leaf Publishing Group, LLC.

ISBN: 978-1-68344-429-9
ISBN: 978-1-61458-948-8 (digital)

All Scripture verses are from the King James Version of the Bible.

Please consider requesting that a copy of this volume be purchased by your local library system.

Printed in the United States of America

Please visit our website for other great titles:
www.masterbooks.com

For information regarding promotional opportunities, please contact the publicity department at pr@nlpg.com.

Profiles of Integrity

1

Real People
Who Demonstrated
Godly Character

Marilyn Boyer &
Grace Tumas Ehrman

Credits

Thanks to the following people for their indispensable help in writing Portraits of Integrity:

Grace Tumas Ehrman, for her sensitive and colorful portrayal of these heroes in writing their stories.

Mary Ann Edman who, with help from her husband Ed, produced the layout and design, along with other beautiful graphic effects. Thanks, Mary Ann, for your commitment to excellence!

And Judy Saunders, Krystyn Walker, and Grace Boyer for their proofreading work.

Chronological Table of Contents

Table of Contents by Character Quality

Introduction

Portraits of Integrity is sure to be a favorite with your family! It contains 40 stories of real people from history who, in the course of their lives, have been placed in situations where their character shone through.

History is best remembered when learned through the stories of those who lived it! For many years, I have given to parents a list of 45 character qualities with Scripture verses to learn what God's Word says about each one. Principles are best learned from practical examples and that is what has given birth to this book.

Through the lives of people, some of whom you have heard of and some you will be meeting for the first time, you will learn how to appreciate character in the lives of others and be inspired to become people of character yourselves. I hope you will be challenged as I have to learn of people who, often at great sacrifice, strove to fulfill their responsibilities in life and as a result left to us a legacy of character!

Psalm 25:21 says "Let integrity and uprightness preserve me; for I wait on Thee." In Psalm 101:2, the psalmist says. "I will behave myself wisely in a perfect way.... I will walk within my house with a perfect heart." In verse 6, "Mine eyes shall be upon the faithful of the land, that they may dwell with me...." In Portraits of Integrity, through stories, you will be "inviting" into your home those who will inspire your family to live a life of integrity!

Read it on your own or to your family, give as a gift, or use it as enrichment for your history curriculum.

Marilyn Boyer

For whatsoever things were written aforetime were written for our learning, that we through patience and comfort of the scriptures might have hope.

—Romans 15:4

Persuasiveness

DEFINITION

Skillfully handling truth
to lead others in a right path

MEMORY VERSE

And when they had appointed him a day, there came many to him into his lodging; to whom he expounded and testified the kingdom of God, persuading them concerning Jesus, both out of the law of Moses, and out of the prophets, from morning till evening.
Acts 28:23

Give Me Liberty

Patrick Henry

Richmond, Virginia
March 23, 1775

March 23, 1775. Over one hundred men with powdered hair and frock coats crowded the narrow pews of St. John's Episcopal Church in Richmond, Virginia. After Governor Lord Dunmore had forbidden the delegates to meet and discuss the "Intolerable Acts" perpetrated by the British Crown, the Second Virginia Convention found church the only suitable and safe place to gather. Glancing about him, Thirty-nine-year-old Patrick Henry could see Thomas Jefferson's flaming red hair, George Washington's

Patrick Henry

strong and somber face, and the fuzzy yellow head of Richard Henry Lee. A murmur went through the room as the delegates whispered in the moments before assembly. He could feel the tenseness, the unease. Nobody was sure what to do about rising pressure in Virginia, memories of the killings in Massachusetts, known as the Boston Massacre, and the humiliation of the tea taxes. Few people wanted to make a sudden move. House delegates stood up, one after another, arguing, jabbering.

Patrick Henry had tried to go into business. When it failed, he took up planting, but his house burned down. Then he struck out in a new line of trade. When that, too, collapsed, he discovered his great love in the law. In 1763, he made a name for himself during the "Parson's Cause," a trial that established that the Virginia Colony, not the British Crown, would determine a minister's salary. He won the case. Later, he burst into the limelight when he tried to beat down the Stamp Act of 1765 with his Virginia Resolutions. He based their complaints on the rights of Englishmen to fair representation. In the middle of his speech, "Caesar had his Brutus; Charles the First his Cromwell; and George the Third—" the Speaker of the House suddenly shouted, "Treason! Treason!" Patrick Henry calmly finished, "—May profit by their example. If this be treason, make the most of it!"

In 1774, as the separate colonies moved slowly but unalterably towards the final showdown, he joined a committee of correspondence. The Committee passed written circulars throughout the colonies and let the citizens know what was going on.

On this March day, men stood and argued. They had still reached no decision. Many things pressed on Patrick Henry's mind today. At home, on his estate in Scotchtown, Patrick's wife Sarah, now in her mid-thirties and mother of six children, lay in the two-room basement, dying. Four years ago, she had started to look at him strangely. Soon she became unable to do simple household tasks or care for the children. When she tried to hurt herself, Patrick had to buckle her into a "Quaker shirt," a straightjacket to keep her safe. He couldn't send Sarah to an insane asylum after almost twenty years of marriage. So he built her an apartment in the basement, full of light and air, with a beautiful view of the trees and the countryside. Every day, he came to see her, bathed her, guided her arms through the sleeves of her dress and combed her hair. Sometimes he held her hands to keep her from hurting herself. Sometimes he just sat with her silently. Today, one of his slaves would take his place while he was in Richmond.

Impatience boiled up in him as the endless talks buzzed on through the afternoon like horseflies. Most of the men wavered, hoping to keep to a middle road and not offend the British. Mainly, they could not decide whether to mobilize against the encroaching British troops or not.

Suddenly, he could stand it no longer. He leaped to his feet.

"Mr. President . . ."

Words poured from his lips. "There is no retreat but in submission and slavery! Our chains are forged! Their clanking may be heard on the plains of Boston! The war is inevitable—and let it come! I repeat it, Sir, let it come." He took a deep breath. "It is vain, Sir, to extenuate the matter. Gentlemen may cry "Peace, Peace"—but there is no peace. The war is actually begun! The next gale that sweeps from the north will bring to our ears the clash of resounding arms! Our brethren are already in the field! Why stand we here idle? … . Is life so dear, or peace so sweet, as to be purchased at the price of chains and slavery? Forbid it, Almighty God! I know not what course others may take; but as for me, give me liberty or give me death!"

They were on their feet now, shouting, "To Arms! To Arms!" Protests rose like bubbles underwater, but soon evaporated under Henry's persuasive language. Mobilization began at once, with Patrick Henry taking the lead as Colonel of the 1st Virginia Regiment. In August, he led the militia in protest when Lord

Dunmore ordered the gunpowder secretly removed from the magazine during the night. In a night of torches and shouting, Dunmore surrendered the powder at the same time the British marched on Lexington. Patrick Henry's efforts, combined with those of Samuel Adams, Paul Revere, and other patriots in Massachusetts, marked the beginning of the war. Later, he served as Virginia's first and sixth post-colonial governor.

Sarah died that spring. Henry planted a lilac tree near her grave that would bloom every spring after her death. Two years later, he married Dorothea Dandridge, who gave him another eleven children. At the Virginia Convention of 1788, he voted against the ratification of the Constitution, preferring to see a Bill of Rights added first. After struggling in vain to get Virginia to endorse and fund a state religion, against Thomas Jefferson's plea for complete religious liberty, Patrick Henry spent his last years on his plantation at Red Hill. He succumbed to stomach cancer in 1799. A failure at business but a success at oratory, his "Give Me Liberty" speech touched off a spark in Virginia that flamed into a

Patrick Henry addressing the Virginia Convention

common movement for independence.

Patrick Henry used persuasive words to convince his listeners to enter the fight for liberty.

Questions

1. Why was the Second Continental Congress meeting in St. John's Episcopal Church?
2. What was pressing on Patrick Henry's mind that day?
3. How did Patrick Henry treat his ill wife?
4. What did Patrick Henry communicate in his speech?
5. How did his persuasiveness influence others to join the fight for liberty?
6. Tell in what manner Patrick Henry became involved with the militia.
7. Think of someone in Scripture who used persuasiveness to influence others for good.
8. List people who are in your sphere of influence whom you could potentially influence for good.

Enthusiasm

DEFINITION

Exercising caution in all situations; foreseeing the consequences of my actions

MEMORY VERSE

A prudent man foreseeth foreseeth the evil, and hideth himself: but the simple pass on, and are punished.
Proverbs 22:3

The Black Robe

Pastor John Muhlenberg

Virginia
January, 1776

Woodstock, Virginia: January 21, 1776. The cold, cracked logs hummed with warmth and a babble of German and English voices. Outside, blue ridges rose over the Shenandoah Valley cloaked in snow. Stepping into his pulpit in the Lutheran meeting house, thirty-year-old Pastor John Peter Gabriel Muhlenberg adjusted his heavy, long black robe. It fit him smoothly from his wrists to his ankles. Framed by a soft white wig, his thin-lipped face gazed over the congregation. Men in homespun breeches and

Pastor Muhlenberg rallying his congregation

women in caps and shawls, with children clinging to their hands, waited in silence.

His eyes moved over their faces, studying each one. The war hadn't touched this valley yet, but drums beat in Massachusetts to the north. Soldiers marched in red waves. It was only a matter of time until the clash came. Last year in the crowded St. John's Church in Richmond, he saw a red-haired man leap to his feet. Gripping the pew in front of him, Patrick Henry shouted: "I know not what course others may take; but as for me, give me liberty or give me death!"

Muhlenberg thought of George Washington's face as he asked him to rally more men to fight. Today, the pastor would leave this valley, and he would take with him the sturdy log walls, the bite of snow in his face, the grip of the tough valley men. But he would not leave them behind. They had not called him "Devil Pete" for nothing when he fought with the dragoons in Germany twelve years before.

Now Muhlenberg raised his head. His voice rang out, strong and clear:

"There is a time for all things: a time to preach and a time to pray, but those times have passed away. There is a time to fight—and that time has come!"

Suddenly, Pastor Muhlenberg threw back his robes. Underneath, he wore the blue-and-buff uniform of a colonel in the Revolutionary Army. His eyes pierced the congregation. Stepping down from the pulpit, Muhlenberg waved his hand. Drums outside the door began to beat. One by one, men stooped to kiss their wives and children. Muhlenberg watched as they streamed into the rough-hewn aisles. His enthusiastic demonstration had worked a miracle. In half an hour, 162 men from three congregations had joined the Continental Army. When Muhlenberg led the 8th Virginia Militia out from Woodstock the next day, the ranks had swelled to 300.

Some historians now argue that mention of Muhlenberg's spectacular disrobing that Sunday in January 1776, is conspicuously absent from all contemporary accounts. While it is not known how much of this story is fact or myth it is certain that Peter Muhlenberg preached a stirring sermon and then marched at the head of his regiment to join the Continental Army.

Next, Muhlenberg headed south to defend the coasts and swamps of Georgia and South Carolina. In 1777, he raced north to support Washington's troops during the bitter winter at Valley Forge. Serving through the fierce battles of Brandywine and Monmouth, Muhlenberg earned the rank of brigadier general just as Washington and French forces under Rochambeau laid siege to Cornwallis at Yorktown. Joining the attack, the enthusiastic preacher-turned-soldier and his men stubbornly held the right flank as Washington's army closed in for the victory. While Lafayette's Light Division trundled cannon through the darkness, Muhlenberg crouched with his men in the trenches, waiting for the signal to attack. On the night of October 14, 1781, Muhlenberg's infantry charged the slopes of Redoubt No. 10 with fixed bayonets. The British lines caved in. Soon, a white flag fluttered over the embankments. Cornwallis had surrendered.

General John Peter Muhlenberg

Muhlenberg's famous robe is still in existence. It resides in the historical collection of the Lutheran Theological Seminary in Philadelphia.

Peter Muhlenberg demonstrated enthusiasm both through his words and actions. As a result, he influenced hundreds of men to fight in one of the first Virginia militias of the war.

There is a time for all things, a time to preach and a time to pray, but those times have passed away. There is a time to fight, and that time has now come.

—General John Peter Muhlenberg

Questions

1. In what part of the country did John Peter Gabriel Muhlenberg preach?
2. What speech had inspired Pastor Muhlenberg about a year earlier?
3. What section of Scripture did he preach on that day?
4. What did he do that surprised his congregation?
5. How many men from his congregation joined him that day?
6. How many men joined him to become the 8th Virginia Regiment?
7. Tell of some of the battles in which he and his men were involved.
8. How did Muhlenberg's enthusiasm influence the men in his congregation?
9. How can enthusiasm for the right things be used to accomplish much good?
10. Think of a way you could be enthusiastic to inspire others to do good for the Lord.
11. How could enthusiasm to be used in your home to help others to cheerfully manage everyday tasks?

Flexibility

DEFINITION

Cheerfully being willing to change my plans when circumstances beyond my control require it

MEMORY VERSE

Be careful for nothing; but in every thing by prayer and supplication with thanksgiving let your requests be made known unto God. And the peace of God, which passeth all understanding, shall keep your hearts and minds through Christ Jesus.

Philippians 4:6-7

Caesar Rodney's Ride

General Caesar Rodney

Delaware
July 1776

July was a time for storms. For uprisings. For revolts. Caesar Rodney, Brigadier General of the Delaware Militia, tore open the note. His eyes quickly scanned the message. It was from the Continental Congress in Philadelphia. His friend, Delaware delegate Thomas McKean, was deadlocked with George Read on the vote for independence. As a Delaware delegate, only the absent Caesar Rodney could break the tie. Would Delaware go to war against Britain or not? The general hesitated.

It was late afternoon. He was tired after a long day spent crushing a Loyalist revolt in Sussex County. The countryside was a nest of Loyalist vipers crawling under his feet. After the hunt, the Loyalists scattered into the swamps. Some boarded British ships and sailed away. Others lay low, masking their hostility. So far, nine colonies had voted for independence, two against, while New York had abstained. Delaware was stuck with a split ballot. And his vote alone could alter the future of the state and the coming war. That decided it. He was a delegate and it was his duty to vote. But the voting began early tomorrow morning in Philadelphia, eighty miles away. Without stopping to eat or change his clothes, he saddled up his horse.

General Caesar Rodney

It began to rain. Caesar Rodney pulled on boots and spurs. He knotted a cape over his shoulders. He looked like a crane, hunched over the horse's neck, slender as a reed, his head swaying gently on his thin neck. Even Molly Vining, the woman he loved many years ago, had never called him handsome. But his face had fire, sense, humor. He galloped out onto the Delaware road. The rain came harder, spattering his shoulders like bullets and churning the dusty summer road to a lake of mud. If this kept up, it would be a challenge to get to Philadelphia in time.

Rodney could not remember a time when he had not been in some public office. Was it twenty-eight years? Twenty-nine? At forty-eight, the years tended to pile in on him, mingling his roles and functions. Registrar of wills, recorder of deeds, clerk of the orphan's court, High Sheriff of Kent County, representative in the colonial legislature at Newcastle, member of the Stamp Act Congress, brigadier general of the Delaware militia and Speaker for the state assembly. He had never married. After Molly Vining rejected him and ran off with a vicar, he had never found anybody else to care for him. He buried himself in his work. His country became wife, family, and child to him. Perhaps it had always been that way.

Forty miles. The rain lashed his face, slanting off the brim of his hat. Lightning split the sky. Thunder crashed against the trees overhead. He could hardly see the road in front of him, swirling with mud and water. July was the time for storms. For war. He planned his speech to the Virginia delegates. They always looked down their noses at the smaller states as if to say, "We'll take care of you. We are the rock on which Independence rests."

Despite the rain running down his neck, Rodney tingled all over. "Let Virginia be of good cheer. . ." Yes, that was the way to put it. "She has a friend in need. Delaware will take her under its protection and insure her safety."

Seventy miles. His thighs ached from the saddle. He was a good horseman, but he had never ridden eighty miles in a storm. The horse staggered; he stopped to change it for another. He could feel the night spinning, turning over into the next day. July 2, 1776. Through the rain he could see the sparse, flickering lights of Philadelphia. Almost all the city lay in grey darkness, waiting for what the morning might bring. Peace or war. In the hall of the Continental Congress, only the delegates were awake. Sitting over candles burned down to nubs, they hotly argued the issue of independence. New York still refused to cast a ballot. Thomas McKean stared down George Read. Neither would budge an inch. The real voting was due to begin any moment now.

Suddenly, there was a clatter of spurs in the hall. Heads swiveled towards the entrance. Tall, soaking wet, and bringing with him the smell of the rain, Caesar Rodney stood in the doorway. He was ready to vote. The ballot he cast that day thrust Delaware decisively into the war and gave Congress the unanimous vote it had been waiting for. He was tired. But not too tired to puncture the egos of the Virginia delegates. Turning towards them, General Rodney said loudly: "Let Virginia be of good cheer . . . Delaware will take her under its protection."

Because Caesar Rodney showed flexibility, he was able to cheerfully change his plans at a moment's notice and ride eighty miles out of his way to cast his vote for independence.

...That these United Colonies are, and of Right ought to be Free and Independent States, that they are Absolved from all Allegiance to the British Crown, and that all political connection between them and the State of Great Britain is, and ought to be totally dissolved.

—Declaration of Independence

Questions

1. Caesar Rodney had already endured a grueling day defeating a revolt. How did he demonstrate flexibility when he received the message upon returning home?
2. Why was his vote so important?
3. How did his vote cast that day affect you today?
4. What hardships did Caesar Rodney endure to get there on time?
5. What other character qualities did he demonstrate besides flexibility?
6. Again, we have a demonstration of the sacrifice of one person affecting an entire world! Why is it so important for you to develop the disciplines of godly character into your life? How can your diligence to learn flexibility now make you a more profitable servant for God?
7. Think of an instance where you didn't want to show flexibility recently. Memorize Philippians 4:6-7 and bring them to mind the next time you are tempted to be selfish instead of flexible.

Honesty

DEFINITION

Speaking the truth in all situations

MEMORY VERSE

Lie not one to another,
seeing that ye have put off
the old man with his deeds.
Colossians 3:9

One Life to Live

Nathan Hale

New York
September 1776

September 21, 1776. He had arrived late at the meeting. Now, Captain Nathan Hale felt Colonel Knowlton's eyes piercing each face in the room, raking his athletic, almost six-foot body, his fair hair, and blue eyes. By the end of June, the British had invaded Long Island. General George Washington, driven towards Harlem River, could barely hold his position. He desperately needed a volunteer officer to slip behind the British lines, obtain accurate information and come back again. "We have not been able to obtain the least information as to the enemy's plans," Washington had declared. But today his officers in their blue-and-buff coats kept silent. Captain Hale saw Colonel Knowlton turn to an experienced French noncommissioned officer.

"Will you go?" he asked.

The Frenchman's lilting voice was grim. "I am willing to be shot, but not to be hung."

Nathan Hale

No one else moved. Captain Hale saw the disappointment in Knowlton's face as he knew that he would have to report his failure to Washington. Suddenly, Hale stepped forward.

"I will undertake it." His face still looked white from his recent sickness.

William Hull, his friend and classmate, tried to talk Hale out of the notion that evening. "Don't go," he warned. "This is not in your line of duty. Besides, you are too frank and open a person to be a spy and face its dangers. It will probably lead to a disgraceful death."

But Hale would not go back on his word. "I want to be useful," he said quietly, "and every kind of service necessary to the public good becomes honorable by being necessary. If the exigencies of my country demand a peculiar service, its claims to perform that service are imperious."

Those were the last words he spoke before he plunged into the unknown. Hull never saw him again. On September 12th, Hale left Sergeant Stephen Hampstead and his servant Asher Wright at camp to take care of his uniform and a few belongings. Then he changed into civilian clothes and rowed across the Hudson to Huntington, or Oyster Bay, not far from Long Island. He carried with him his college diploma, certifying him as a Connecticut schoolmaster visiting New York to look over the schools. By crossing over into British-held territory, he had committed an act of spying punishable by immediate death. At Oyster Bay, he told the boatman to come back for him on October 20th. Avoiding detection, he at last reached New York.

Suspicion ran high in the city. The great fire raged through New York City, consuming a quarter of the lower part of Manhattan. British troops, wading through smoke-blackened debris, suspected that American saboteurs had set the fire as Washington retreated towards the northern tip of the island known as Harlem Heights. Others believed that the British themselves set torches to homes and buildings in an attempt to frighten the few patriots still left in the city. The Provincial Council had taken down all the bells used to ring the alarm from the churches. The fire engines refused to work. Sir William Howe, stationed at his headquarters in the Beekman Mansion, began rounding up and jailing more than 200 Americans as suspects.

In Manhattan and Long Island, Hale passed straight through the British army. He made detailed sketches of the fortifications and made notes on their number and various positions.

As Captain Hale sat in a New York tavern one day, his Loyalist cousin Samuel Hale and Major Robert Rogers of the Queen's Rangers glanced across at him. They saw straight through the disguise and recognized him as one of Washington's officers. Introducing himself to Hale, Major Rogers lured him into a friendly chat. He claimed to be a secret patriot himself.

On October 20th, Hale returned to the secluded spot at Flushing Bay near Queens, New York, where he had left the boatman a week before. He gave the signal and the boat swung towards him. Too late, he saw that it came from a British frigate lying offshore and screened by a thick fringe of trees. Rogers and his Rangers caught up with Hale before he could run.

They took him to Beekman Mansion, standing on a rise at the head of Turtle Bay, where Howe waited for them. Inside the house, the British searched Hale thoroughly. They found the maps, sketches, and incriminating notes—written in Latin—hidden in the soles of his shoes. Hale did not try to dodge. He admitted his name and rank. According to eighteenth-century protocol, the military leaders of both sides considered spies as illegal combatants worthy of death. There was no trial. Howe gave orders to execute him next morning.

Hale spent the night of October 21st in a glass-sided greenhouse on the property, in the hands of the brutal Provost-Major, William Cunningham. As night wore away towards dawn, Hale begged Cunningham for a Bible. The request was denied. A little later, the captain asked to speak to a clergyman. Again, Cunningham turned him down. Early the next morning, Captain Montresor, an English officer stationed nearby, asked permission to let the American captain sit with him in his tent while making his final preparations. On entering, Hale asked for paper, quills, and ink. Montresor gave them gladly. Captain Hale sat down and wrote two letters, one to his mother and one to a brother officer. But the letters never arrived. Cunningham, seizing them from the prisoner, destroyed them on the spot. He didn't want the rebels to know that one of their men could die with "such firmness."

Nathan Hale signaling his boatman

The final march began. Hale walked under guard along the Post Road until they came to the Artillery

Park between Rutger's orchard and the Dove Tavern. As his captors prepared to execute him for treason, Nathan Hale lifted his head.

Captain Nathan Hale being prepared for punishment

"I only regret that I have but one life to give for my country."

Several of the British officers watching later noted that the captain had a gentle dignity about him. His face was calm, his voice firm as he spoke. He was twenty-one years old.

Over a century later, Edward Everett Hale, Nathan Hale's great-nephew, declared: "And because that boy said those words, and because he died, thousands of other young men have given their lives to his country."

Nathan Hale demonstrated honesty by owning up to his identity as a spy. As a result of his refusal to lie, the entire Continental Army was inspired by his example.

Questions

1. What job did Colonel Knowlton need a volunteer to do?
2. Why was Nathan Hale willing to volunteer?
3. How did he go about his mission? Did he acquire the information?
4. How was he discovered?
5. What were the conditions of his capture?
6. What did Nathan Hale request of his captors? Did he get his request granted?
7. What words did Nathan say just before his death?
8. How did he demonstrate honesty, knowing what his fate would be?
9. How was Nathan Hale's honesty used to inspire others?
10. How can you demonstrate honesty every day? List some examples of times you've been honest/dishonest. What were the consequences of both?
11. What verse can you learn to bring to memory when tempted to be dishonest?

Generosity

DEFINITION

Giving unselfishly to
the needs of others

MEMORY VERSE

Give, and it shall be given unto you; good measure, pressed down, and shaken together, and running over, shall men give into your bosom. For with the same measure that ye mete withal it shall be measured to you again.

Luke 6:38

Dead Money

Robert Morris

Philadelphia, Pennsylvania
December 1776

"The Hessians are coming!" On an icy December day in 1776, a rider burst into the calm session of the First Continental Congress. General Howe, massing 30,000 troops, had attacked Cooper's Ferry opposite Philadelphia with an army of kilted Highlanders and fierce, German dragoons.

Forty-two-year-old Robert Morris, head of a rich merchant firm and signer of the Declaration of Independence, was on his feet, his massive and dominating body squeezed into a dark silk suit. His

Robert Morris

square face, with its powdered grey hair tied loosely behind, looked grim. While the members rushed home to pack for Congress' retreat to Baltimore, John Hancock, with a price on his head, turned to three delegates and gave them last words of advice. Robert Morris, with Clymer and Walton, would remain in the blighted city to carry on the work of Congress.

Now one day later, Morris was alone. Standing in the empty Congress hall, Morris watched the two men leave and hurriedly cross the street. Moving to a table covered with papers, inkwells, and feather pens, he picked up an authorized bill. With it, he must borrow $10,000 for the defense of the Marine Committee. His wide, sensitive mouth tightened. Now to see to the barricades across the Delaware.

From where he stood, he could not see the broad grey expanse of water, perfect for shunting a fleet of warships across to fire on Philadelphia. With a dark cape thrown over his shoulders, Morris emerged into the street. Beds, furniture, and trunks teetered on the sidewalks as panic escalated in the city. Only the Quakers were staying—and Robert Morris.

For three months, Robert Morris was to represent

the scattered Congress. He served as chairman of the Finance Committee. He sent daily reports to the President of Congress. As head executive, he authorized loans, signed documents, served as intelligence officer, warden of the port of Philadelphia and directed the construction of the first Continental Navy. His grey hair blowing in the wind, he strode through the shipyards urging men to work faster, shoring up defenses and inspecting fire-rafts along the Delaware, forcing the pace on shipbuilding and repair. Day and night he knocked on doors, borrowing money for the cause. Inflation rose sharply, creating "dead" money by the bushel, while housewives fed fires and papered their walls with Continental currency.

As new demands rained down on him, Morris put the dying money to work. "There are no carpenters." "The crews will desert unless they are paid." Again, he dug into his own pocket to shell out wrinkled Continental bills. George Washington needed 150 pounds to pay his spies; the Marine Committee was deep in debt. Morris borrowed in silver, repaying in gold.

Then at sundown on December 31, 1776, a messenger galloped up to Morris' door. He brought an urgent letter from General Washington at Trenton. He needed $50,000 immediately. Howe intended to cross the Delaware and capture Philadelphia as soon as the river froze over. Without pay and with their enlistment time up, Washington's ragged troops were on the brink of desertion. By sheer willpower and the promise of $10.00 bonuses, Washington had managed to keep his men from deserting for another six weeks. But he was not sure he could hold them that long.

Could Morris get the money? Morris tossed all night, his mind racing. This was the biggest demand yet. The treasury was empty. He had already given all of his own money to Congress. But he never dreamed of refusing Washington. Early morning sunlight filtered through the windows. Robert Morris dressed quickly. As New Year's Day broke over the city, Morris set off towards the Quaker residential section. He rang the doorbell at his friend Abel James' house. "What news so early, Robert?" The Quaker looked startled.

"The news is this, my friend." Morris' cheeks looked ruddy with cold. "Washington needs a sum of money and I must send it to him immediately. I would like you to lend me $50,000."

Abel James hesitated. "But what is thy security, Robert, for this large sum?"

Morris stared straight into his friend's eyes. "My word is my honor."

"Thee shall have it," the Quaker replied quietly.

Pen in hand, Morris wrote to Washington: "Sir, I am up very early this morning to dispatch a supply of $50,000 to your Excellency." The troops reenlisted. On the night of January 3, 1777, Washington's troops crossed the Delaware and defeated the British at Princeton, saving Philadelphia.

Robert Morris continued to serve till the end of the war. His generosity and skill in finance enabled him to rescue his country at a crucial time in history, earning him the title "Financier of the American Revolution."

In accepting the office bestowed on me (Superintendent of Finance), I sacrifice much of my interest, my ease, my domestic enjoyments, and internal tranquility. If I know my own heart, I make these sacrifices with a disinterested view to the service of my country. I am ready to go still further; and the United States may command every thing I have, except my integrity, and the loss of that would effectually disable me from serving them more.

—*Robert Morris*

Questions

1. What caused people to flee from Philadelphia? Why did Robert Morris stay?
2. What earned Robert Morris the title of Financier of the Revolution?
3. What functions did Robert Morris perform while in Philadelphia?
4. Who depended upon him to raise money to supply the army?
5. What was the special need that arose on December 31, 1776?
6. How much money did Gen. Washington need?
7. How did Robert Morris obtain the money?
8. For what purpose was the money used?
9. What campaign was won with the use of that money? What effect did this have on freedom you now enjoy?
10. How did Robert Morris exemplify generosity?
11. What opportunities do you have to practice generosity in your home? In your church? In your community?

Attentiveness

DEFINITION

Listening with the ears, eyes, and heart

MEMORY VERSE

The ear that heareth the reproof of life abideth among the wise.

Proverbs 15:31

The Listeners

Lydia Darragh

Philadelphia, Pennsylvania

December 1777

The winter twilight was closing in. Time to light the candles at No. 177, the tall brick house on the corner of South Second and Little Dock Streets. For Lydia Darragh, wearing a white Quaker bonnet, it seemed as if the British had occupied Philadelphia forever. In reality, they had come in September 1777. It was now December 2nd. Just across the street loomed the big house that held General William Howe's headquarters. All at once, the parlor door opened.

"Major André." Lydia smiled warmly.

The British spy was trembling with suppressed excitement. Late tonight, he and a number of high-ranking British officers would converge on her house for an important meeting.

"And be sure, Lydia, that your family are all in bed at an early hour. When our guests are ready to leave the house, I will give you notice, that you may let us out and extinguish the fire."

He knew she would do it. As she swept the upstairs room, her mind reverted to André's words. The British were planning something full-scale. Where was Charlie tonight, her oldest son? Encamped at Whitemarsh with the 2nd Pennsylvania Regiment of the Continental Army.

It was 8 p.m. With her children asleep, Lydia softly slipped off her shoes. The house was deadly quiet. Light glimmered under the door of the conference room as the small woman crouched in an adjoining linen closet. A murmur of voices. Then came the clipped accents of General Howe. He was reading aloud an order. On the night of December 4th, British troops were to secretly evacuate the city. According to his spies, the Americans planned to move camp. The British would then ambush them at Whitemarsh, slaughtering them in the open fields.

Oh, God. Charlie was at Whitemarsh. Pressing her ear to the wall, she listened, scarcely breathing. The voices flickered, died down like embers in the fire. Lydia crept back to bed. Almost immediately, someone hammered on the door. Lydia lay rigid. She knew André was out there. Heart pounding, she lay

Lydia Darragh

staring into the dark. As the blows continued, she got up and let the officers out into the night. André remarked that she must be a sound sleeper. He had had to knock three times. Back in bed, Lydia's thoughts tormented her. This was not the first time she had engaged in espionage. On her trips through British lines, she carried a sewing kit. Copying a message onto a tiny slip of paper, she sewed it into her clothing or concealed it beneath a button.

As dawn broke over the city, Lydia crossed the street to Howe's headquarters and obtained a pass to go to Frankford to buy flour. Trudging the eight miles on foot and carrying an empty sack, Lydia appeared at the Rising Sun Tavern. Elias Boudinot, Commissary of Prisoners, was busy eating breakfast. Lydia came up to him with a question about flour and instead thrust a dirty needle-book into his hands. Surprised, Boudinot flipped through the pockets until he came to the last one. There, he found a slip of paper. Unrolling it, he learned that Howe was coming with 5,000 men, 13 cannons, baggage wagons, and eleven boats on wheels. Boudinot (with Colonel Craig, also at the Rising Sun) galloped at once to

Washington's headquarters. When the British attacked on December 4th, the Americans turned the tables on Howe's army at Edge Hill. On December 9th, Major André summoned Lydia Darragh to headquarters. His face was grim.

"Were any of your family up, Lydia, on the night when I received company in this house?"

"No," she replied. "They all retired at eight o'clock."

"It's very strange." André mused. "You, I know, Lydia, were asleep . . . Yet it is certain that we were betrayed. I am at a loss to conceive who could have given the information of our intended attack to General Washington! . . . We found [him] so prepared at every point to receive us, that we have been compelled to march back like a parcel of fools. The walls must have ears."

Only Lydia Darragh knew. Having learned to listen attentively and accurately, Lydia Darragh was able to prevent a British victory at a crucial time. If Washington's army had been destroyed at Whitemarsh, it is possible that the founding of America might have taken a very different turn.

Though we consider thee as a public enemy, we regard thee as a private friend. While we detest the cause thee fights for, we wish well to thy personal interest and safety.

—Lydia Darragh

Questions

1. What did Major André instruct Lydia and her family to do that evening?
2. Where did Lydia go to attentively listen to the British plans?
3. Why did the British think Lydia was a sound sleeper?
4. What was an extra motivation for Lydia to want to help the American cause?
5. How did Lydia deliver her message and to whom?
6. What was the outcome of the British advance on Whitemarsh?
7. How did Lydia Darragh's attentiveness contribute to the advancement of freedom?
8. How can you practice attentiveness when your parents speak to you? When you are listening to the preacher in church? When a friend is sharing his experiences or burdens with you?

Availability

DEFINITION

Being willing to attend to a need
when I am called to help

MEMORY VERSE

Also I heard the voice of the Lord,
saying, Whom shall I send,
and who will go for us?
Then said I, Here am I; send me.
Isaiah 6:8

Sergeant Molly

Molly Pitcher

Battle of Monmouth
June 1778

It was so hot that the men were dropping by the roadside like flies. Twenty-four-year-old Molly Ludwig Hays craned her neck, looking for John. Where was he? He ought to be with the gunners near Wenrock Creek at Monmouth, where American Generals Stirling and Greene withstood the forces of Clinton. Sweat beaded her forehead as she scanned the smoky battlefield, sharp bayonet points glittering in the sunlight. Cannon blasts shook the ground.

Across the field, John stooped over a gun in Captain Alexander's Company of the 7th Pennsylvania Regiment. Dark hair pulled smoothly back into a queue, face browned by the sun. He worked relentlessly, ramming home cannonballs, lighting the tow fuse, loading again. British grenadiers, pushing to cross the causeway, staggered back under the heavy fire. As long as the cannons kept firing, the Americans stood a chance to win. Molly shifted the pitcher to her other hand. Hitching her skirts high, she began to move towards him. As a camp follower, trailing her husband from camp to battlefield, Molly had learned lessons in availability. She also knew how to change her plans at a moment's notice and serve when needed.

A moan to her right. Behind her. To her left.

"Water. Water."

Tattered Continental soldiers lay gasping on the scorched ground. Molly hesitated, glancing towards John. The heat was killing. Grasping her pitcher, she ran to a nearby spring. Water bubbled out of the ground. Filling her pitcher to the brim, she moved back along the lines. The men could see her coming from a distance, a tall, broad-shouldered young woman in a white neckerchief, her sleeves rolled up to the elbow, stepping carefully between their dusty feet.

They began calling to her: "Molly! Pitcher!"

The name stuck. Again and again she refilled her pitcher, lifting their heads, spilling cool water down their burning throats. The temperature soared to over 100 degrees. General Stirling's cannon, barely holding the causeway, wavered between the advancing British and Washington's desperately regrouping troops. Wounded men fell, blocking the gunners' feet as the cannon rocked backwards with each explosion. Suddenly, Molly saw her husband slump to the ground. His face was pale and clammy. Molly knew the signs all too well. Heatstroke. He was alive, but unconscious. She stood up. Just then, a Colonial officer rode up to the cannon. He ordered it pushed back out of the way to make room. There was simply no man left to fire it.

Molly Pitcher

"I can do it." Molly Pitcher straightened up.

The officer stared at her, tangled hair, smudged cheeks, skirt tucked high up above her calves. This woman looked like she could do it. And she was actually offering to help. He nodded and rode away. Molly grabbed the smoking-hot ramrod—a wet rag tied to the end of the long pole—and rammed it deep into the barrel. She swabbed out the sparks and gunpowder residue. Then she packed in cannonball, powder, and cotton wadding, driving home the ramrod swiftly, accurately. She blasted away into the massed Redcoats struggling on the bridge. This is for John. This is for John. Once, a British cannonball shot between her legs as she bent over the cannon, tearing away a large piece of her skirt.

Molly glanced down and laughed. "Well, that could have been worse."

The soldiers roared appreciatively; she had become one of them. Molly continued to swab and load as the hot Sunday afternoon faded into dusk. It grew darker; the firing lessened. The British troops pulled back in defeat, leaving their wounded, and the exhausted Americans withdrew into the ravine. General Washington, seeing Molly Pitcher from a distance, personally commended her and gave her the rank of sergeant. Some of the men began calling her "Sergeant Molly." In 1822, ten years before her death, the House of Representatives voted to pay Molly Pitcher $40 annually for the rest of her life, "for her services in the Revolutionary War." Her name has since appeared on a postage stamp, a World War II ship was christened for her, and a stretch of US Highway 11 in Pennsylvania is known as the Molly Pitcher Highway.

Molly Pitcher did not look for fame when she carried water and manned a cannon at the Battle of Monmouth on June 28, 1778. She was simply available, open to the opportunities that came her way to serve in a time of need.

Whatsoever thy hand findeth to do,
do it with thy might….

—Ecclesiastes 9:10

Questions

1. What was Molly Hays doing at the Battle of Monmouth?
2. What job was her husband John performing?
3. How did Molly demonstrate availability to the parched soldiers?
4. What happened to John that prevented him from continuing his job?
5. How did Molly demonstrate availability when John was unable to proceed?
6. What was George Washington's response on seeing Molly engaged in battle?
7. In what ways was Molly honored for her sacrifice to the American cause?
8. How can you demonstrate availability in your home? List some ways.
9. Who in Scripture was available to meet a need when they became aware of it?

Decisiveness

DEFINITION

The ability to make wise, deliberate decisions based on God's standards

MEMORY VERSE

But let him ask in faith, nothing wavering. For he that wavereth is like a wave of the sea driven with the wind and tossed.

James 1:6

Sea Monsters

Captain John Paul Jones

English Coast
September 1779

Thursday, September 23, 1779. It was 3 p.m. when he first sighted them. A light southwest breeze scudded across the waves off Flamborough Head, forcing the two warships to drift closer. Leaning on the rail of the *Bonhomme Richard,* thirty-two-year-old John Paul Jones peered through the haze at the heavy British frigate *Serapis.* His blue coat, embroidered with gold epaulets, shone in the sunlight. His square jaw was taut, his brown hair pulled smoothly back from his brow. Behind him bunched the masts

Captain John Paul Jones

of his own four ships. He had had his eyes on the *Serapis* for hours. This was the ship he had waited so long for. At first, the sea was smooth as glass. Then as he doubled back, looking for prizes at the mouth of the Humber River, he caught sight of the British frigate running straight up the Yorkshire coastline from the Baltic Sea. A dozen ships fanned out behind the *Serapis* like a peacock's tail. They were merchant ships, en route from Scandinavia, rolling with supplies: rope, canvas, timber.

At 1 p.m. the British sighted Jones' cluster of ships drifting below the chalky cliffs of Flamborough Head. Flags began signaling: "Strange sail in sight." Jones knew it was time to act to cut the enemy supplies off from the English coast. Among his four ships, Jones could muster 120 guns, capable of smashing over a thousand pounds of metal into the *Serapis*. But Jones' ship was old and slow, tired from cruising the seas. The *Serapis* was brand new, twice as fast and able to outmaneuver Jones' ship like a spider in a dance. A victory would not only cut the lifeline to Britain's "wooden wall"—the Royal Navy—but it would also secure him lasting fame.

Cruising towards each other, the vessels made no more than a mile or two an hour. At 5 p.m. the warships were so close that the deck of the *Bonhomme Richard* was cleared for action, chairs and tables thrust down into the hold to reduce the danger of flying splinters. Sailors sprinkled sand over the deck so it would not turn slippery with blood.

The late summer evening was soft and still light. Hazy clouds spread over the North Sea. At 6:00, Jones ran up his flags. Blue. Blue. Yellow and blue. They signalled "Line of Battle." The flags shivered in the wind. Glancing back, Jones saw his own ships, the *Vengeance* and the *Alliance,* veer away. The *Pallas* tacked off on her own course, her sails bright in the fading September sunlight. He was suddenly alone.

Now the British man-o-war was so close he could see her yellow topsides bellying up above the water. The smaller sloop huddled closely in her wake. Aboard the *Bonhomme Richard,* crews dragged chains and braced the yards, while the gun crew crouched over the 18-pounders, holding lighted matches aloft as the breeze drove the ships slowly inwards. Someone let out a joke. And the crew was roaring with laughter when the ship rocked with the first broadside from the *Serapis* a moment later. Two of Jones' guns burst, killing most of the crew nearby. Within minutes, his heaviest armament was out of action. Lieutenant Richard Dale, grimy with gunpowder and spattered with sweat, found Jones up on deck. The captain wheeled around.

"Dick, his metal is too heavy for us! He is hammering us to pieces. We must close with him. Bring your men on the spar deck and give them the small arms."

Seamen swarmed up into the rigging with pistols to take out the enemy gunners from above. The risk was great. A single spark from a flintlock weapon could blow the entire powder magazine sky high. Shells crashed into the hull, staving in the old East India merchant ship's sides. But Jones instructed the men to clear the *Serapis'* rigging of British and then sweep the decks. By 6:00, the sun began to sink behind the white cliffs of Flamborough Head. The *Countess of Scarborough* ran in along Jones' port side, scalding him with gunfire. Just then, the captain of the *Pallas* realized that Jones was fighting, not surrendering. He reversed his direction and rushed back to help.

Six miles away on Flamborough Head, an excited crowd watched as the ships foamed and struggled like sea monsters in the waves below. Darkness fell, and the stars came out, pricking the black sky. In the east, a harvest moon, big and orange as a cannonball, came up out of the sea. The ships' shapes were still clearly visible, but not their flags.

Suddenly the hoarse voice of Captain Pearson bellowed into the dusk: "What ship is that?"

Jones thought quickly: *"The Princess Royal."*

Both ships were East-Indiamen and roughly the same size. But Pearson was not satisfied.

"Where from?"

Jones kept silent.

"Tell me instantly whence you came and who you be, or I'll fire a broadside into you!"

Jones saw that the game was up. He scrapped his false Royal colors and ran up the Continental flag. Without warning, both ships erupted into gunfire.

A red glare spread over the sea. Many of the ships were on fire. Ropes, masts, and splintered yards littered the decks. The ships were only twenty-five yards away now, blasting away with the concussion of 42 cannons. Officers, standing exposed on the deck, steeled themselves not to flinch as shot whizzed past them. At this point, Captain Pearson determined to finish off this bold American. He slid out from under the ship's lee (a protected position from the wind) and prepared to rake the bow with gunfire. And then, the wind died. This was Jones' chance. The *Serapis* hung just off to starboard, unable to move an inch.

"Well done, my lads," he shouted. "We have got her now!"

He leaped forward with a line to lash the two ships together. The sailors grabbed cutlasses, pikes, and pistols and prepared to board the enemy ship. They scrambled forward, clutching at the bowsprit, as the Royal Marines peppered them with musket balls. It was impossible. Slipping on the wet deck,

Jones called back the attacking party. But the wind was shifting in his favor. Slowly, Jones drove the ship in closer until it lay across the enemy's bow. If he angled it into correct focus, he could rake the *Serapis* from stem to stern. The *Bonhomme Richard* was barely moving now. The smoke was so thick that Jones could barely see the cartridge wads from the British guns smoldering in the shattered masts. The gun room, filled with the badly burned, was abandoned. The boat began to sink below the waterline as the ship's carpenter, up to his chin in water, fought to stop the flow with canvas and wooden plugs. But the pumps were too slow.

He shouted aloft: "We're sinking!"

Two mates and an English officer on board heard it. Jones, they believed, was dead, lost to sight in the billowing smoke and darkness. They ran for the mainmast and began to lower the last American flag. Sailors panicked as the ship pitched and tilted beneath them. Suddenly, Jones heard the cry of "quarter!" He lunged across the deck at the culprits, bringing up his pistol, just as Pearson leaned over the rail and shouted: "Have you struck? Do you call for quarter?"

The whole world grew still. The British, almost invisible in the darkness, his own bloody and smoke-grimed men, the prisoners manning the pumps below, all waited for his reply.

Then John Paul Jones shouted: "Struck, sir? I have not yet begun to fight!"

It was 10 p.m. Four hours had passed since the *Serapis* first fired on the *Bonhomme Richard.* Then the miracle happened. A Scotsman scrambled onto the *Serapis'* platform in the darkness and began lobbing grenades across the ship's deck. Explosions rocked the British vessel. Two-ton guns blew from their carriages, somersaulting in the air. The ship was on fire in a dozen places and men began leaping into the sea. It was now 10:30 p.m. Jones, hunched over a nine-pounder twenty yards away, saw Pearson's stiff figure appear on the ladder to the deck.

"Sir, I have struck!" Pearson shouted. "I ask for quarter!"

The battle was over.

Because John Paul Jones exemplified decisiveness and made wise decisions, he was able to tie two ships together and win the battle for the American Revolution.

I wish to have no connection with any ship that does not sail fast; for I intend to go in harm's way.
I have not yet begun to fight.

—John Paul Jones

Questions

1. What was the mission John Paul Jones set out to do?
2. What was the name of his ship? What was the name of the British frigate?
3. What was the business of the British frigate?
4. Describe what happened during the battle.
5. What was Jones' reply when asked if he was surrendering.
6. What decision did Jones make that won the battle?
7. What is the definition of decisiveness?
8. Think of a situation when you or someone you know demonstrated decisiveness to bring about a good result.

Alertness

DEFINITION

Being keenly aware of what is taking place around me so I can be prepared with a right response

MEMORY VERSE

Be sober, be vigilant; because your adversary the devil, as a roaring lion, walketh about, seeking whom he may devour.

I Peter 5:8

The Virginia Giant

Peter Francisco

The Carolinas

August 1780

August 15, 1780. It was hot tonight, as hot as those dim, barely remembered nights on the blue island in the Azores. Sometimes, when he closed his eyes, he could see the green lawns with the mansion in the background, his sister playing, and the sound of a father's language he did not know. Now Private Peter Francisco, of Colonel William Mayo's Virginia Militia Regiment, paced on guard duty as the moon gradually wore thinner, like pirates' fingers rubbing away at gold pieces of eight. At age twenty, he stood over six-foot-six and weighed 260 pounds. He had attacked Stony Point beside "Mad" Anthony Wayne, survived the Battle of Trenton, and been hospitalized at Valley Forge. Now the war was moving south. Already, Savannah and Charleston had fallen to the British. General Gates, raising a new army to fight in the Carolinas, determined to surprise the superior British forces with less than half the number of men.

The last thing Peter Francisco heard was the familiar rustling and chirping of birds as they stirred and woke to the dawn. Suddenly, Cornwallis' cavalry broke over the sleeping militiamen like water over a dike. The raw recruits scrambled to their feet, fleeing the redcoats' bayonets and trampling hooves. All but Peter. As the terrified men burst through the ragged line of Continentals, General Gates wheeled his horse and galloped from the field.

Wounded soldiers, bogged-down cannons, and thrashing horses littered the road. Peter thrust his bulk here and there, trying to stop the tide. But the men streamed past him, rolling frightened white eyes. Glancing around quickly, Peter caught sight of a small cannon abandoned between the Virginia and North Carolina Militia lines. It weighed 1,100 pounds. He couldn't leave it there, a sitting duck to aid the British. Hoisting it to his broad shoulders, he carried the field piece to a nearby position where Continental gunners wheeled it back towards the enemy. The battle was almost over, with barely a struggle. Peter

Peter Francisco

slipped into a wooded area, as two of Colonel Banastre Tarleton's cavalrymen came screaming at him through the trees.

They were almost upon him now. But he kept still, holding his empty musket butt up, sideways, in a gesture of surrender. Then as the Redcoat leaned down to seize the gun, Peter swung it with all his might, cracking the man across the skull. A quick bayonet thrust at the other cavalryman sent him crashing to earth. Grabbing a sword from the ground, Peter swung onto a horse and galloped off. Just ahead, his own Colonel Mayo was trudging along, surrounded by a cordon of guards: a prisoner. Prepared to act, Peter charged. He cut down both British guards and slapped a horse towards his astonished officer. Peter later complained that his swords broke like "toothpicks" during the battle. Far away in Pennsylvania, George Washington heard stories of this Virginia private and ordered a six-foot-long broadsword forged for him.

But nothing could tie Peter down to one battle or one experience. Gripping a horse with his thighs, bearing down on an enemy, the wind in his face—the incidents at the Battle of Camden left Peter Francisco itching to join the cavalry. In 1781, he got his chance.

British resistance in the Carolinas was weakening after the battles at King's Mountain and Cowpens. Peter Francisco, recovering from a leg wound at Guilford Court House, returned to the army to act as scout against the notorious British cavalryman, Colonel Tarleton. As night drew on, he stopped at Ward's Tavern (West Creek Tavern) in the wilds of Nottoway County to rest. As he leaned on the bar inside, nine Tarleton dragoons silently encircled the inn. Peter was trapped. Tarleton's men stripped him of his weapons and dragged him outside. The moon was up, and Peter could clearly see that they left only one man on guard. Most of the thirsty dragoons clattered into the tavern to drink in celebration. The guard leered at his silver shoe buckles.

"Take them off and hand them over," he ordered.

Peter's lips curled.

"Take them off yourselves if you want them," he dared.

Someone made a grab for them. And in that instant, Peter moved like a black panther. With a single bound, he twisted the guard's saber from his grip and struck him down. Inside, the other redcoats heard the uproar. A dragoon rushed out into the yard to see what was happening, his white doeskin breeches gleaming, crimson shell jacket flaming like blood. He shot from the steps, a bullet hitting Peter in the side. As his body went numb, then hot, Peter sprang at the dragoon with his saber. Then the brawl began.

He was whirlwind, fire, danger. The violent events of his young childhood flooded his mind.

He was five years old again, playing on the lawn of a shadowy island palace, when rough hands seized him from behind. He heard his sister scream. Then she was kicking, scratching, breaking free. A cloth tied over his eyes. A gag stuffed into his mouth. His arms and legs bound. Then blackness. The slow, rolling heave of a ship. The keen smell of salt. Sometimes he listened to their voices from where he lay. The voices he had heard in the night. Were they pirates? Friends who had abducted him to keep him safe from the dark mystery that surrounded his parents? Why did he understand his mother's fluent French, but not his father's unknown tongue? Then the splash of oars. The sultry silence of a June day in 1765 broken by the sounds of a boat moving away from the pier at City Point, Virginia. Footsteps along the boards, then voices. Where am I? Strange, suntanned faces bend over him. He sees their tattered shirts, their tarry pigtails. Dock-workers? He doesn't know. He looks up at them, a sturdy little boy with an alert brown face. He chatters excitedly. Trying to tell them. They brought me here. What is this place? But the words don't come out right. They don't understand. He tries Portuguese, Spanish, French. He sees them glance at each other. He shows them his clothes, the tattered aristocratic linen coat trimmed with lace, his gleaming silver shoe buckles that form the letters "P" and "F." "Pedro Francisco," he shouts desperately as he is taken away to the poorhouse. "My name is Pedro Francisco. I belong to somebody." Maybe that is what he had been trying to do all his life. To prove that he was someone.

Peter was never quite sure how many dragoons he killed or wounded at Ward's Tavern. Three or four crawled on hands and knees or lay still. Another soldier aimed a musket at him. He heard the dry click as he lunged for the musket, knocking it out of the Redcoat's hands. The man slipped sideways to the ground, and Peter forked his legs over the horse. Shots from the lighted tavern followed him as he galloped off into the night, leading a string of eight horses.

The incident became known as "Francisco's Fight," winning him the title the "Virginia Giant." George Washington would later claim: "Without him, we would have lost two crucial battles, perhaps the war, and with it our freedom. He was truly a one-man army."

In the years following the war, Peter Francisco married three times and fathered six children. At his plantation Locust Grove in Buckingham, Virginia, he wore the bright clothes of a southern planter, hunted, fished, and threw parties where he entertained guests with his fine tenor voice. In 1953, Virginia dedicated March 15 as Peter Francisco Day. Wounded six times during the Revolutionary War, he is the only enlisted man in the Continental Army honored with a holiday.

A park, a bicentennial United States postage stamp, and a fiddle tune bear his name. The dress sword given to him in appreciation by Colonel Mayo was presented to the Virginia Historical Society, but has been lost to history.

Because Peter Francisco demonstrated alertness, he overcame superior forces to save his own life and the lives of those around him during the crucial years of the Revolutionary War. While his story is rarely found in history books, his awareness of what was taking place around him enabled him to be prepared with a right response

Without him we would have lost two crucial battles, perhaps the war, and with it our freedom. He was truly a One-Man Army.

—quote attributed to George Washington

Questions

1. Tell what occurred on August 15 as Peter Francisco was standing guard.
2. What acts of incredible bravery did he show?
3. How did he come to be surrounded at Ward's Tavern?
4. What did he do when the dragoon tried to steal his buckles?
5. What memory did getting shot trigger in his mind?
6. How did he escape? What did he take with him?
7. What won him the title of "Virginia Giant"?
8. What did George Washington say about Fransisco?
9. How through practicing alertness did he save his own life and others as well during the Revolutionary War?
10. Think of some opportunities you have to demonstrate alertness.
11. How might alertness help you to be a better babysitter or helper to your younger siblings?

Discretion

DEFINITION

Avoiding any words, actions, or attitudes that could give the appearance of evil

MEMORY VERSE

The proverbs of Solomon the son of David, king of Israel ... to give subtilty to the simple, to the young man knowledge and discretion.

Proverbs 1:1, 4

Race to the Dan River

General Nathanael Greene

Virginia
February 1781

They moved under cover of darkness, horses, wagons, and men. Thirty-eight-year-old Major General Nathanael Greene, his large figure looming in the saddle, watched from the bank at Boyd's Ferry as Continental soldiers streamed past, torchlight gleaming on their straggling hair, exhausted faces and torn, grimy uniforms. Greene moved with a heavy limp. He cocked his ear, listening intently. On winter nights like these, sound traveled for miles. The clink of a saber or the rattle of military accoutrements

General Nathanael Greene

would sound like a gunshot in the darkness. Melting snow and rain splashed underfoot, creaked under the wheels of the gun caissons, fell with a soft plop into the Dan's frigid waters. It seemed as if the whole world was hushed in wet snow.

Just two months before on December 2nd, Congress had chosen Greene, Quartermaster General of the Continental Army, to replace the ineffective Horatio Gates in command in North Carolina. The war for the South hung in the balance. Robert Howe lost Savannah. Benjamin Lincoln surrendered Charleston without a fight. And in August 1780, Horatio Gates' army ran in wild confusion from the Camden battlefield. In despair, Washington wrote to Greene of his decision to select a new general for the southern theatre. He ended: "It is my wish to appoint you." Known as the "Fighting Quaker," Greene would win a reputation as a hero of the army.

Facing Cornwallis' well-armed and superior forces, Greene decided to divide his troops. According to military books, this was the wrong thing to do. Dividing troops into two wings weakened an army's central core and lessened its punch effect. But Greene did it anyway. By splitting up his own troops, he forced the British to split as well. The gamble paid off with the American victory at King's Mountain. All at once, the war shifted in favor of the Revolution.

The race started the day after Cowpens, when Greene sent General Daniel Morgan into South Carolina with one wing of the army. The day Cornwallis forgot to look behind him and found Morgan crashing into his rear. After luring British cavalry under Colonel Banastre Tarleton away from any hope of reinforcements, Morgan closed in, decimating nine-tenths of the British troopers and capturing over 800 men. Cornwallis spun like a tiger. His one goal: to free the redcoat prisoners and destroy the rebel army before it could reach safety in Virginia. Greene knew what was going on in Cornwallis' mind. The British commander hoped that Morgan, retreating towards Salisbury with a clutch of booty, would not be able to link up with the brilliant and discerning Nathanael Greene. The ragtag army began their run before dawn. Cornwallis, camped near Ramseur's Mill, burned his wagon train and started after them.

If the Continentals could reach Virginia and the main body of the army, they would be safe. Greene, receiving urgent messages from Morgan, swiftly swung his wing north to join him. Greene set off in the grey dawn with three dragoons and a guide. The damp, cold air pressed in on them. Stealthily, they glided through the bleak countryside of Anson County, zigzagging to avoid detection by British foraging parties until they came upon Morgan's hidden position. The next day, a rainy Thursday, Greene, Morgan, General William Davidson of the Salisbury District Brigade of North Carolina Militia, along with Colonel William and Captain Joseph Graham sat huddled on a log in the raw weather a few hundred yards from camp to trace their next moves. Greene shrewdly calculated their resources. He had only Morgan's "flying army" (mobile and strategic troops) and Davidson's 600 militiamen to face Cornwallis' pursuit. He spoke seriously.

Cowan's Ford

Morgan would hold the upper ford, Sherrald's Ford. Davidson would move farther down to guard the lower fords at Beattie's Ford, Cowan's Ford, and Toole's Ford. When he could hold it no longer, he would fall back to Salisbury for shelter and supplies. Greene knew that they could not stay there long. Cornwallis, only a few hours behind them, scouted out the fords at the Catawba. He saw that Morgan held Sherrald's Ford in force, while Davidson strongly defended Beattie's. Cornwallis sent a feinting attack towards Beattie's Ford, while he shifted downriver to capture Cowan's Ford. Davidson guessed what had happened. In the ambush and skirmish that followed, Davidson fell mortally wounded. When several discouraged patriots withdrew to Tarrant's Tavern, cavalrymen under Tarleton followed them there and cut down ten of them.

On Thursday evening, his troops wet and tired, their powder soaked from the rain, Greene slipped by Tarrant's Tavern several hours before Tarleton arrived. While his men loaded wagons with food, ammunition, and weapons, Greene dashed off letters to General Huger and "Light-Horse Harry" Lee, asking them to come to his aid. He had already written Patrick Henry for more troops, adding, "In all probability, you will find me on the North side of Dan River . . . I [will] in turn race Lord Cornwallis as he has done me." Early Saturday morning, in driving rain, Greene watched from horseback as his men slogged through the rapidly rising Yadkin River.

The race began. Pushing their prisoners in front of them, they avoided the few roads that existed. They waded through deep creek-beds and struck out across muddy fields under torrential skies. Cornwallis, paddling across the Catawba, regrouped on the other side and rested all day. Meanwhile, the Continentals kept marching. Greene kept the British frustrated and guessing which direction he had gone. He formed a special operations group under Colonel Otho Williams to spy out British movements and cover the main army's retreat. On February 6,

Morgan reached Guilford Courthouse in a steady downpour of rain and sleet, while Cornwallis kept up the hunt for him within a radius of twenty-five miles. Greene arrived the next day, and the two wings of the army joined again. The result numbered a paltry 2,036 exhausted and hungry men.

Now they approached the Dan River. They had been on the march for almost three weeks, a deadly race that brought them out of the rolling hills of North Carolina to this broad, menacing stretch of icy water. Beyond them lay the flat lowlands of Virginia—and safety. Colonel Williams, ordered to stall or distract the British at any cost in order to facilitate the crossing, galloped with his cavalry just ahead of the van of the British army.

As they neared the end of their run, Greene sent out urgent messages to every ferryman in Halifax and Pittsylvania Counties: "Bring every boat you can find." A flotilla of rafts and little

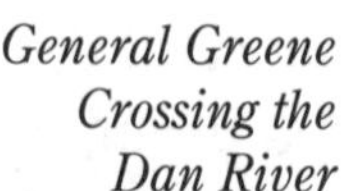

General Greene Crossing the Dan River

fishing boats appeared out of nowhere. On Tuesday, February 13th, they began crossing in the darkness at Boyd's and Irvine's Ferries, dragging animals and equipment through the bone-chilling water. Mass after mass passed on the boats, faces streaked in the torchlight, the cannons bobbing and the horses swimming. Other soldiers hunkered behind hastily constructed earthworks ready to fight the British off if they came pouring down the bank. The "light" troops skittered along behind, fighting off skirmishes on the slippery, muddy roads, destroying bridges and interrupting British intelligence. The last of Greene's men clambered up the opposite side.

The British outriders, close behind them, could hear the sound of voices and see the flickering torches. But they could not reach them in time. Cornwallis arrived on the banks of the Dan at 8 o'clock on Thursday morning. It was Valentine's Day, the river was running high, and all of the boats had gone. Balked, Cornwallis could not cross. The three-week race over 250 miles of rainy and sleet-covered roads, fighting off attacks and crossing major rivers had ended. Safe on the other side, General Greene slept for a few hours before pushing deeper into Virginia. By avoiding a pitched battle with his men in a weakened condition, Greene conducted one of the greatest strategic retreats in history. Collecting fresh troops, he turned back into North Carolina to face Cornwallis again at Guilford Courthouse.

General Nathanael Greene demonstrated discretion by carefully weighing his situation and deciding on the wisest course of action, first by dividing up his troops and then by choosing to retreat rather than plunge into a fight.

America must raise an empire of permanent duration, supported upon the grand pillars of Truth, Freedom, and Religion, encouraged by the smiles of Justice and defended by her own patriotic sons.

—Nathanael Greene

Questions

1. What position in the Continental Army did Nathanael Greene hold?
2. Why was the south in such bad straits?
3. What decision did Nathanael Greene make that defied military advice?
4. What was Greene's strategy?
5. How did he end up executing his plan?
6. How did the retreat turn out?
7. In what way did Greene demonstrate discretion?
8. Think of a situation where you acted without first weighing the situation and making a wise decision. How did it turn out? If given a second chance, what would you do differently?
9. Think of someone in Scripture who acted with discretion and tell how God's purposes were accomplished as a result.

Selected Bibliography

Andreyev, Ivan. *Russia's Catacomb Saints: Lives of the New Martyrs*. California: Saint Herman of Alaska Press, 1982.

Bashkiroff, Zenaide. *Nights Are Longest There: A Young Girl's Account of Revolution in Russia*. London: M. Spearman, 1960.

Berkin, Carol. *Revolutionary Mothers: Women in the Struggle for America's Independence*. Vintage Press, 2006.

Bruce, Philip Alexander. *Brave Deeds of Confederate Soldiers*. Harrisonburg: Sprinkle Publications, 2006.

Caldwell, Charles. *Memoirs of the Life and Campaigns of the Honorable Nathaniel Greene, Major General in the Army of the United States and Commander of the Southern Department in the War of the Revolution*. Philadelphia: Robert Desilver, printer, 1819. Reprint. Nabu Press, 2010.

Callo, Joseph. *John Paul Jones: America's First Sea Warrior*. Naval Institute Press, 2006.

Cheripko, Jan. *Caesar Rodney's Ride Eighty Miles for Freedom*. Boyd's Mill Press, 2004. (Grades 3-6).

Davis, Burke. *To Appomattox: Nine April Days, 1865*. N.Y: Rinehart & Company, 1959.

Delaplaine, Edward S. *Francis Scott Key: Life and Times*. Heritage Books, 2011.

Driggs, Laurence La Tourette. *Heroes of Aviation*. Little, Brown and Company, 1918 (Armand Pinsard).

Elliot, Elisabeth. *A Chance to Die: The Life and Legacy of Amy Carmichael*. Revell Press, 2005.

Fluckey, Eugene. *Thunder Below! The USS "Barb" Revolutionizes Submarine Warfare in World War II*. University of Illinois Press, 1997.

"The Flying Panther: Captain Edward J. Simpson." American Aviation Society, 2011.

Fougara, Katherine Gibson. *With Custer's Cavalry*. Iyer Press, 2007.

Franklin, Benjamin. *Benjamin Franklin's Autobiography*. W.W. Norton & Company, 1986.

Franks, Norman, and Harry Dempsey. *Nieuport Aces of World War I. Osprey Aircraft of the Aces, No. 33*. Osprey Publishing, 2000 (Armand Pinsard).

Gaustad, Edwin S. *Liberty of Conscience: Roger Williams in America*. Judson Press, 1999.

______________. *Roger Williams*. New York: Oxford University Press, 2005.

Gilmer, George R. *Sketches of Some of the First Settlers of Upper Georgia, of the Cherokees, and the Author*. New York 1855, 1926, p. 90 (Reprinted in 1965 by Genealogical Publishing Co., Baltimore, and 1989 by Heritage Papers, Danielsville, Georgia).

Goodyear, Robert C. *The Real Pennsylvania Dutch American, "Molly Pitcher": A Documented History*. Author House, 2012 (Suggested reading).

Grack-Koestler, Rachel A. *Molly Pitcher: Heroine of the War for Independence*. Chelsea House Publications, 2005.

Green, Roger. *The Life and Ministry of William Booth: Founder of the Salvation Army*. Abingdon Press, 2006.

Hattersley, Roy. *Blood and Fire: The Story of William and Catherine Booth and the Salvation Army*. New York: Doubleday, 2000.

Hearn, Chester G. *Tracks in the Sea: Matthew Fontaine Maury and the Mapping of the Oceans*. International Marine Press, 2003.

Hembree, Charles R. *From Pearl Harbor to the Pulpit: The Dramatic Story of Captain Fuchida and Jacob DeShazer*. Akron: Ohio, Rex Humbard World Wide Ministry, 1975.

Hocker, Edward W. *The Fighting Parson of the American Revolution: A Biography of General Peter Muhlenberg, Lutheran Clergyman, Military Chieftain and Political Leader*. Philadelphia, PA: Edward W. Hocker, 1936.

Holt, Rackham Vincent. *George Washington Carver: An American Biography*. New York: Doubleday, 1963.

Hull, Michael D. "Peter Francisco: American Revolutionary War Hero." *Military History Magazine*, July-August, 2006.

Kackley, Paul. "The Dead Yank Hero of Orleans Forest." *Stars and Stripes*, 25 Nov. 1959.

Kalpaschnikoff, Andrei. *A Prisoner of Trotsky's*. New York: Doubleday Page, 1920.

Kidd, Thomas S. *Patrick Henry: First Among Patriots*. Basic Books, 2011.

Knight, Lucien. *Georgia's Landmarks, Memorials, and Legends*. Penguin Publishing, 2006 (Nancy Morgan Hart).

Lewis, Meriwether. *Original Journals of the Lewis and Clark Expedition, 1804-1806*. New York: Arno Press, 1969.

Littauer, V. S. *Russian Hussar*. London: J. A. Allen, 1965.

Marks, Lara. "Sacagawea as an Evolving Symbol of *American Indian Women*." Dec. 16, 1998.

Marshall, Charles. *An Aide-de-Camp of Lee*. Kessinger Publishing, 2007.

Muhlenberg, Henry A. *The Life of Major-General Peter Muhlenberg, of the Revolutionary Army*. Philadelphia: Carey and Hart, 1849.

Perry, John. *Sergeant York: His Life, Legend and Legacy: The Remarkable Untold Story of Sergeant Alvin C. York*. Barnes and Noble Books, 1997.

Phelps, M. William. *Nathan Hale: The Life and Death of America's First Spy*. Thomas Dunne Books, 2008.

Polsky, Michael. *The New Martyrs of Russia*. Montreal, Brotherhood St Job Pochaev, 2002.

Ramage, James A. *Grey Ghost: The Life of Colonel John Singleton Mosby*. University of Kentucky Press, 2009.

Rappleye, Charles. *Robert Morris: Financier of the American Revolution*. New York: Simon & Schuster, 2010.

Salisbury, Gay and Laney Salisbury. *The Cruelest Miles: The Heroic Story of Dogs and Men in a Race Against an Epidemic*. New York: W. W. Norton & Company, 2005.

San Souci, Robert D. *Kate Shelley: Bound for Legend*. Dial Books for Young Readers, 1995.

Scott, Jane. *A Gentleman as Well as a Whig: Caesar Rodney and the American Revolution*. University of Delaware Press, 2000.

Scott, John Thomas. "Nancy Hart: 'Too Good Not to Tell Again.' " *Georgia Women: Their Lives and Time*s, vol.1. Chirhart, Ann Short, and Betty Wood, Ed. Athens: University of Georgia Press, 2009.

Silcox-Jarrett, Diane. *Heroines of the American Revolution: America's Founding Mothers*. Scholastic, Inc., 2000 (Lydia Darraugh).

Skeyhill, Tom. *Sergeant York and the Great War*. The Vision Forum, Inc., 1998.

Snow, William P. *Lee and His Generals*. New York: The Fairfax Press, 1982.

Strachey, Lytton. *Queen Victoria: An Eminent Illustrated Biography*. New York: Black Dog & Leventhal Publishers, 1998.

Summers, Julie. *The Colonel of Tamarkan: Philip Toosey and the Bridge on the River Kwai*. London: Simon & Schuster, 2005.

Thomas, Evan. *John Paul Jones: Sailor, Hero, Father of the American Navy*. New York: Simon & Schuster, 2003.

Vaughan, David J. *Give Me Liberty: The Christian Patriotism of Patrick Henry (Leaders in Action)*. Cumberland House Publishing, 2002.

Walker, Gary C. *Civil War Tales: Volume II*. A & W Enterprise, 1994.

Washington, Booker T. *Up from Slavery*. New York: Dover Publications, 1995.

Waters-Power, Alma. *Virginia Giant: The Story of Peter Francisco*. New York: E.P. Dutton, 1957.

Wellman, Sam. *George Washington Carver: Inventor and Naturalist*. Barbour Publishing, 1998.

Wetterer, Margaret K. *Kate Shelley and the Midnight Express*. Scholastic, 1990.

Williams, Roger. *A Plea for Religious Liberty in: The Bloudy Tenant of Persecution*. Providence, Rhode Island: Narragansett Club, Vol. III, 1867.

Wrangel, Peter N. *Always with Honor*. New York: Robert Speller and Sons, 1957.

Websites

"Bill Overstreet." http://www.cebudanderson.com/billoverstreet.htm

"Bill Overstreet, 363rd FS." http://www.cebudanderson.com/overstreet.Htm

"Bill Overstreet: Barnstormers." http://www.barnstormers.com/eFLYER/2009/061-eFLYER-FA02-Legends-Overstreet.html

Winstead, Jane. "Horatio G. Spafford: The Story Behind the Hymn 'It is Well with My Soul.' " http://voices.yahoo.com/horatio-g-spafford-story-behind-hymn-is-1620793.html?cat=38.

Image Credits

Alertness

Peter Francisco: Public Domain. Society of the Descendants of Peter Francisco: www.peterfrancisco.org/photos/

Attentiveness

Lydia Darragh: Public Domain. Library of Congress: [Lydia (Barrington) Darragh, 1728?-1789, bust portrait, facing left] Digital ID: (digital file from b&w film copy neg.) cph 3b01548 http://hdl.loc.gov/loc.pnp/cph.3b01548

Availability

Molly Pitcher: Mary Ludwig Hays McCauley AKA "Molly Pitcher" Painting by C.Y. Turner: globalgenealogy.com/globalgazette/gazsh/gazsh-0059.htm

Decisiveness

John Paul Jones: U.S. Senate paintings John Paul Jones by George Bagby Matthews, http://www.senate. gov/artandhistory/art/common/image/Painting_31_00012.htm

Discretion

Nathanael Greene: Public Domain. http://en.wikipedia.org/wiki/File:Greene_portrait.jpg. Original portrait painted from life in 1783 by Charles Wilson Peale

Battle of Cowan's Ford: No author information. http://en.wikipedia.org/wiki/File:Cowansford.jpg

General Nathanael Greene Crossing the River Dan: http://etc.usf.edu/clipart/55900/55956/55956_greene_dan.htm

Enthusiasm

Pastor John Muhlenberg: http://explorepahistory.com/displayimage.php?imgId=1-2-28C Courtesy of the Lutheran Theological Seminary at Gettysburg, Photography by Sara Mummert

Muhlenberg portrait: Public Domain. http://www.ok-safe.com/Black-Regiment-Pastors.htm

Flexibility

Caesar Rodney: Illustration by Linda J. Linder in For You They Signed by Marilyn Boyer, 2009.

Generosity

Robert Morris: Public Domain. Painting by Gilbert Stuart, Philadelphia, 1795

Honesty

Nathan Hale: All images: Public Domain. http://ushistory-images.com/nathan-hale.shtm

Persuasiveness

Patrick Henry: Public Domain. http://en.wikipedia.org/wiki/File:Patrick_henry.JPG

speech: http://en.wikipedia.org/wiki/File:Patrick_Henry_Rothermel.jpg

About the Authors

Marilyn Boyer is the mother of fourteen children, all home schooled from kindergarten through high school. Her passion to train up her children in the character of Christ led her to create Character Concepts Curriculum, a character curriculum for kids of all ages to equip parents in raising children of integrity!

Her many character resources, as well as books on homeschooling and Christian parenting, are available online.

About the Authors

Grace Tumas Ehrman holds a degree in history from Liberty University. Her paper, "Warlords and Samurais: Japanese Interventionists in Siberia During the Russian Civil War, 1918-1922," won an award at the 2013 Phi Alpha Theta History Conference. She specializes in American and Russian history.

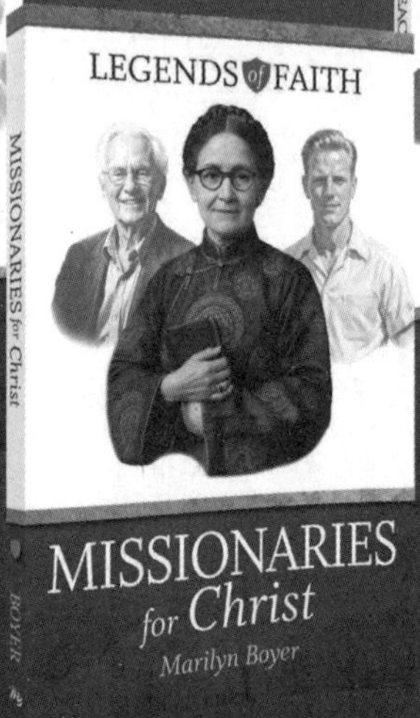